simple

stamps & stencils

♥ style ♥

simple
stamps & stencils

♥ style ♥

S A C H A   C O H E N

Photographs by Lucinda Symons

WATSON-GUPTILL PUBLICATIONS/NEW YORK

Acknowledgements

Thanks to Lucy Fanthorpe and Suzanne Carter for styling,
to Steve Gott and Jon Self for making up the sets
and to Joss O'Brien for assisting.

Published by MQ Publications, Ltd.
254-258 Goswell Road, London EC1V 7EB

First published in the United States in 1998
by Watson-Guptill Publications,
a division of BPI Communications, Inc.
1515 Broadway, New York, NY 10036

Library of Congress Catalog Card Number: 98-60303

ISBN: 0-8230-4807-1

Series Editor: Ljiljana Ortolja-Baird
Editor: Jane Warren
Designer: Bet Ayer
Photographs: Lucinda Symons
Stylist Diana Civil

Printed in Italy

1 2 3 4 5 6 7 8 9/06 05 04 03 02 01 00 99 98

contents

introduction

♥

The creative urge exists in all of us. It may be denied expression by the more pragmatic activities of our hectic lifestyles, side-tracked by lack of confidence and tight budgets, or obscured by time, nevertheless, we have all known the thrill of making something beautiful. But for many of us, our efforts in grade school were the pinnacle of our creative success, and the thought of applying long-forgotten glueing, painting, cutting and drawing skills to the decoration of our homes merely inspires a phone call to that much-recommended, reputable (and reassuringly expensive) interior decorator.

It need not be so. Even the least "crafty" among us can create stylish decor, using the simple techniques of stencilling and stamping. With these techniques, as with our earliest creations, the accent is on individuality and freedom of expression. No right and wrong, but a whole world of possibilities in between. Just as your wardrobe, photo album and garden differ from everyone else's, so should the decor of your home, reflecting the tastes and personalities within. The joy of stencilling and stamping is knowing that your creations are unique, and no amount of catalogue browsing will allow their duplication.

Simple Stamps & Stencils Style introduces the beginner to projects which are simple, both in their design and their execution. Each is well within the capabilities of the average person, and the materials required are the sort that we all have ready access to: paint, brushes, masking tape and the like. The reader already familiar with the art of stencilling and stamping will find these pages brimming with fresh ideas sure to rekindle his or her enthusiasm.

As with other elements of simple style, in the use of stencilling and stamping, less is definitely more. There is nothing worse than the overkill of covering every spare surface and object with some decoration. A light touch is essential here. Used with restraint, simple stencilled designs will enhance the tranquility of the home, whereas a riot of designs will compete with each other to clutter the visual space. On any particular piece, if the question arises "Should I repeat the design again – or add another?", the answer should be "no". It is better to err on the side of subtlety, and you can always add to the design later, if you feel the urge!

Stencilling and stamping have been used as an art form for many centuries. The Egyptians were using stencil art to embellish their mummy cases as long ago as 2500 B.C., but it may have been the Chinese who first adopted the concept of using repeating patterns, as early as 3000 B.C. Since the earliest forms of stencils were fashioned from perishable materials, including leaves, bark and skin, the exact origins of the process are obscure. Fiji islanders traditionally used bamboo and banana leaves for their stencils; the Inuit people of Baffin Island used dried sealskin; while in the Far East, varnished mulberry bark produced a more durable stencil, excellent for printing on fabric. In Japan, stencilled silk had become highly sought-after by A.D. 600, but even the poorest folk employed the technique to decorate their cotton clothing and, by the eleventh century, even Samurai armor boasted intricate stencilled patterns. With the spread of this art via the silk and spice trade routes, stencilling was absorbed by the culture of each adoptive country. Thai stencils reflected largely the local flora and fauna, Indian patterns favored geometric designs and the superb Persian designs depicted tales sacred to their culture. With the dawn of printing in fifteenth-century Europe, stencils were used to add color to woodcut illustrations and in the production of playing cards. Block printed (stamped) fabric was first imported from India into Europe in the mid 1600s. Early, formalized flower patterns in the subdued hues provided by plant dyes (mainly *madder*), were later vitalized by the advent of blue and yellow dyes. Stencilling reached a peak in Europe in the nineteenth century, when the technique was employed to decorate wallpaper, walls, fabric and furniture. In the New World, nostalgic settlers decorated the walls, furniture – and especially floorcloths – of their homes using remembered patterns from the Motherland. Perhaps the first interior designers were the travelling artisans who trundled about New England with their brushes, pigments and stencils, plying a new trade in home decorating!

In Britain, stencilling is among main paint techniques now enjoying a revival. When the Art Nouveau designs of Charles Rennie Mackintosh burst upon the scene at the end of the 1900s, (having been commissioned for that famous Glasgow meeting place Miss Cranston's Rose Tree Tea Rooms), the ancient art of stencilling was rejuvenated and brought into the glare of the twentieth century.

This book is divided into five chapters, each of which focuses on a potential "canvas" for your stencilling and stamping creativity: fabric, furniture, walls, floor and accessories. The projects within each chapter have been chosen for their simplicity and adaptability. Bearing in mind the elements of simple style – function and style – and applying personal tastes and color schemes, the reader can adapt any of these projects to suit their own environment. The ideas shown here may be mixed and matched, applied to a different object in a different setting, or merely used as the creative spark to initiate other original project ideas – the possibilities are limited only by the imagination.

Every room of the house can benefit from the judicious use of stencilling. In the kitchen, the lettering and labels idea is perfect for organizing your food storage jars, and either of the checkerboard designs make a cheerful – and practical – floor treatment. The striking monogram project is a great way to personalize a hallway or formal dining room; the tulip wall frame, quite attractive enough to stand alone, makes more of a wall sconce or treasured painting, and the bathroom is the perfect setting for our fresh, mosaic tile-effect table and nautical floor design. The sanctuary of the bedroom is enhanced by delicate designs and calm color schemes, epitomized here by the ice poppy linen and feather-motif curtains. We probably all own items of furniture which could do with a "face lift", and there is something particularly pleasing about turning a drab and neglected piece into something really special. The chest of drawers, blanket chest and chair projects featured give you the simple means to do just that.

Each project has been specially chosen or designed with speed and a limited budget in mind. Even the most complex projects, such as the checked stamped floor, table linen and blanket chest are well within the scope of a weekend's work, while applying the stencilled or stamped designs to the curtains and bed linen will take no more than a couple of hours.

The art of stencilling and stamping is an easy, effective and rapid way of personalizing and beautifying your home; best of all, it's fun!

INTRODUCTION

floors

The downtrodden floor – often disregarded in our enthusiasm for choosing the colors, fabrics and furnishings for a room – is nonetheless a vital element in the decorative scheme of things. From the understated wall-to-wall carpet in neutral tones through rustic or high-tech tiles and vibrant scatter rugs to the warm honey tones of varnished floorboards, the floor is a potential source of both visual quietude and stimulation. It provides visual continuity between rooms in an open plan home and is often the link which allows an eclectic mix of styles in a room to work successfully. Unfortunately, the other characteristic of all floors is their uncanny ability to collect dust, mud, and food spills. In high-traffic areas, particularly in homes with young children, the visual link between rooms may at times be

provided by a trail of unwelcome mud! For this reason, practicality and durability is a high priority when it comes to choosing a floor finish. Wooden floors are my personal favorite; I love the texture, grain and warmth of the wood, and, best of all, they are very easy to keep clean. Wooden floors are also versatile, and, given the right attention, can be used in virtually any part of the home. They can be sealed or varnished, painted. stained or whitewashed and, of course, they make a wonderful "canvas" for stencilling and stamping designs. With floors, you can be quite bold with the color and scale of your design – the size of the area is quite liberating – but avoid too many "repeats" and steer clear of fussy designs.

A border stencil is often all you need to transform the room, and it may be wise to first sketch your design on a floor plan before you begin. Other than that, stencilling or stamping floors couldn't be easier, as you will see from the four suggested projects in this chapter: a cool green "gingham" floor; a floor stamped in colorful checks; a whitewashed floor with drifts of autumn leaves and a bathroom floor given a fresh, nautical look.

FLOORS

checked stamped floor

Painting wooden floor boards is the simplest way of decorating a floor. You can choose from a huge range of colors and, when you decide to redecorate the room, you can simply repaint the floor for a very modest outlay. From a practical point of view, the painted floor is hard to beat; a soft broom and a wet mop are all you need to keep it clean and, of course, a new coat of paint will refresh the floor at any time.

If you would like something a bit more decorative, then using a stamp to create a pattern on your floor couldn't be easier. For this floor, I have used simple square stamps to apply an unusual combination of yellow/cream and lilac/mauve to achieve an overall checked effect. A plain yellow rug complements the floor pattern beautifully.

▶ 15

Left: Detail of the colorful
stamped floor.

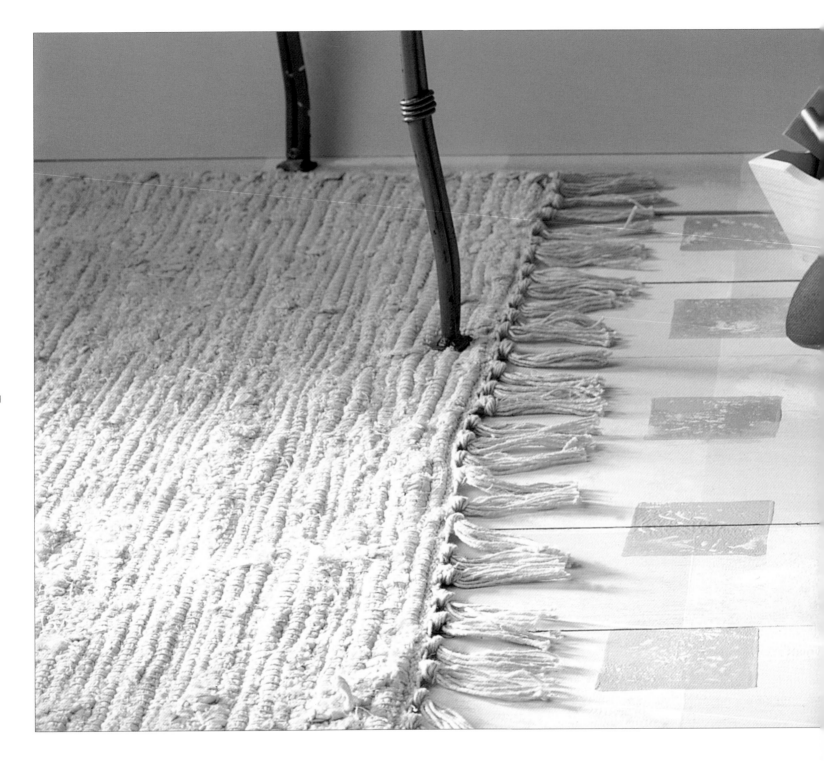

FLOORS

leaf stamped
whitewashed floor

Bring the outdoors in with a seasonal theme – this unusual floor finish is an ideal choice for a den or sun room that overlooks the garden or where uncarpeted areas are the most practical solution.

Bare floorboards need not be dull, as this unusual stamped border shows. In this project, which involves first stamping on the design and then coating the floor with a whitewash, you have the chance to be creative with matte and gloss finishes, contrasting one against the other to highlight the natural grain and finish of the wood.

Natural images are uncomplicated and restful to the eye – their use suggests a warmth of color and complements neutral shades in a room.

Close-up showing two leaf print details.

green gingham floor

♥

There are gingham curtains, gingham tablecloths, gingham chair covers – why not then, a gingham floor? The characteristic elements of gingham are perfect for a wooden floor: the repeating, regular pattern of squares; the simple white base color teamed with green; the freshness, simplicity and the practicality of the design. Once I'd decided to make a gingham floor, I couldn't wait to get started.

Creating the gingham design involves three easy stages. The width of the floorboards determines the size of the checks, and the floorboards themselves provide a convenient straight edge. Stripes in green are stippled first in one direction, and then the other (at 90° to the first). Lastly, the intersections of the stripes are emphasized using a square stencil and a darker shade of green. Of course, you could choose to use two different colors, to create a "tartan" effect, but bear in mind the unavoidable combination of colors at the intersections.

Detail showing mottled effect of stamps.

FLOORS

nautical rope twist floor

♥

Choose a fresh color scheme for your bathroom, where cleanliness is a top priority. Blues and greens and maritime themes – especially fish and shell motifs – are popular for obvious reasons, but there is enormous scope for individuality here. In fact, the ceramic and glass world of baths, showers and basins can be a lifeless one, crying out for color, focus and interest. If you have been wondering where to hang a quirky print, or where to display that unique first attempt at a ceramic "bowl," then look no further, for if there is one room in the house which can accommodate a sense of humor, it is the bathroom.

I have given this floor a nautical look with a border stencil in a rope twist design. The stencil is not painted in solid color, but rather gently stippled along its edge, to create the impression of shading and the desired three-dimensional effect.

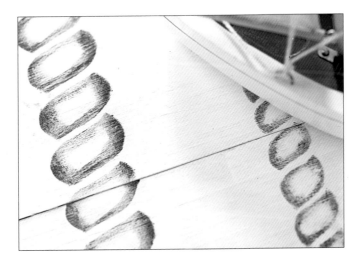

Close-up showing the shading effect of stencilling.

walls

The choice of wall treatments and finishes is almost infinite. Besides the standard coat of paint, there are thousands of wallpaper designs to choose from, as well as the options of using fabric or wood panelling, in order to achieve your desired effect. If, like me, the thought of wallpapering a room brings back unpleasant memories of earlier attempts when your initial enthusiasm was rapidly replaced by frustration, don't despair. You need not be confined to a lackluster world dominated by jaded creams and off-whites; instead, you can introduce color and life into your rooms using simple paint techniques, stamps and stencils.

Before painting, first determine the effect you want to achieve. This will depend on the function of the room. A formal living room will have different requirements from a child's playroom or the guest bedroom. Do you want the room to have a calm, restrained atmosphere, or is the accent on fun and spontaneity? Next, make a note of those features of the room which you might like to accentuate, such as an alcove, or an unusual window.

In most rooms, the walls act as a foil for the other decorative elements of the room: the curtains, furniture and accessories. In this case, a subtle paint effect or simple stencilled design work best. In other rooms, the decorative treatment of the walls is integral to the theme of the room. Children's rooms, for example, come alive with stencilled characters from favorite stories, while a row of stencilled botanical "framed prints" in a bathroom make a practical alternative to pictures obscured behind misted-up glass.

In this chapter, I have chosen four different projects to illustrate the diversity of stencilling and stamping: an illumination-style monogram; a cool white-on-blue spiral design; a picture panel with a two-color tulip design and a unique wall finish which I discovered, quite literally, by accident.

WALLS

spiral
wall finish

♥

The quiet elegance of a restrained color scheme appealed to my desire for a restful and calm interior when I made my first outline sketch for this room. A cool matte blue mottled background offset with a crisp white stencil effectively creates an atmosphere of peace and tranquility.

The symmetry of a repeating curling scroll and rosette motif gives a classical look, adding focus and interest to the wall without jarring the eye. This understated style blends into the background, providing the canvas against which the furniture and soft furnishings are allowed to become the focus of attention.

The scroll pattern appears like a rosette when viewed close up.

plaster spot
wall finish

♥

As with many things in life, an accident can lead to the discovery of a great idea. This was indeed the case with this project. The handle of my paint roller fell into the bucket of drying plaster. Having wiped off the plaster, I stood the roller on its end on newspaper to dry, unaware that the handle had a half-inch indentation in which the plaster had settled. Some hours later, I removed the roller from the newspaper. The plaster in the handle had slid onto the paper and dried, leaving a perfect circle. This technique can be applied to any surface and is a good solution when a very subtle finish is required.

An end of a small roller is a perfect stamp and the handle provides adequate pressure to emboss the mixture.

initial letter
monogram

♥

The art of illumination – the practice of adorning text with intricate illustrations which tease the eye, then reveal the capital letter at the beginning of a chapter – has always held a fascination for me. Perhaps the special appeal of this ancient art is the unique combination of consummate skill and attention to detail, the vibrant palette and the extravagant, often fanciful, interpretation of a single letter.

This design for an initial monogram, although much simplified, was inspired by the art of illumination. Stencilled in two colors, the letter and frame design has a three-dimensional look, and the details picked out in gold lend a sophisticated touch. The design looks dramatic against a backdrop of a strong base color, as here. When you have finished this most unusual method of personalizing your walls, just sit back, relax – and wait for a guest to ask you the name of your decorator!

Two stencils were used to create this
design – a solid background overlaid
with colorful details.

tulip
wall panel

♥

Make more of a treasured antique wall sconce or a painting by creating this unusual frame. Alternatively, in the right setting, this design is strong enough to stand alone: you could coax an awkward alcove from the shadows with this kind of attention, or you could try repeating the panel along a wall in a very large room for dramatic effect.

In each instance, it is important to first consider the proportions of the panel in relation to the wall and the room, and then scale the design up or down as needed. Also, it is advisable to carefully mark out the panel using a level before you begin painting, to avoid disappointment later on.

Close-up showing tulip detail.

fabric

▶ 39

Over many centuries, fabric has been stencilled and stamped for use as window dressings, wallhangings, clothing and floorcloths. The wide range of fabric available to us today only serves to increase the possibilities.

Most fabric will accept a stencil, but, for the beginner, there are a few things to bear in mind when choosing cloth. For clear results, choose fabric which is closely woven, without a glaze (like chintz), and without surface texture. However, for those who like to experiment, textured fabrics can create unusual broken patterns in the stencil design. Expensive does not necessarily equal best; inexpensive, natural fabrics such as muslin, cambric, denim,

and curtain lining, are all excellent In fact, it is always wise to practice on scrap fabric first. In general, self-design will be lost on a patterned stencilled successfully. The New obvious example and creating a a clever disguise for the wear and zones. Carpets with a pile are not or stamping.

bases for stencil and stamp work. techniques and color combinations colored fabrics are best; a stencil fabric. Even floor coverings can be England floorcloth is the most colorful floorcloth effect can be tear, spills and ills of high-traffic a suitable base for stencilling

In this chapter, I have chosen four projects which are striking, yet surprisingly simple to make: natural linen tablecloth and napkins, stamped and stencilled with a seashell motif; fresh Egyptian cotton bed linen delicately sprinkled with ice poppies; a sumptuous velvet pillow, stencilled and braided and curtains with a feather-light design in a contrasting color.

These projects rely on color contrasts and simple designs for their dramatic effect. Remember that the color of the base fabric may alter the color used for the stencil, so, to avoid disappointment, be sure to test your color combination out on a scrap of fabric before you begin.

FABRIC

FABRIC

feather stencilled curtain

♥

In a crisp combination of blue and white, these curtains make a striking statement which belies their simplicity. The feather motif is delicate, but, if used with a strong fabric color, they would not look out of place in the kitchen, bathroom or bedroom. This is perhaps the easiest of the projects included in this book, but a particular favorite of mine. The beauty of the design lies in its calm simplicity. With too many repeats of the feather stencil, these curtains would become fussy, quite the opposite of the look achieved here. By placing the stencils carefully, using a light touch and exercising some restraint, your aim should be to achieve a calm, floating-feather look.

Close-up of one feather design.

ice poppies
bed linen

♥

Stamping on fabric is one of the easiest and most immediate ways in which to enliven and personalize bed linen. Choose quality white Egyptian cotton sheets, duvet cover and pillowcases. A good 100 per-cent cotton fiber will accept and fix the paint readily. It will also wash and wear well, giving you many years of use. For the stamp design, select a single small- to medium-sized motif – one that will work well with the furnishings in your room. Spend time and be careful in selecting the right motif as it will be with you for the life of the bed linen. The general rule for stamping of "fewer is better" also applies to bedding. Avoid a pat-tern which is too busy: personalizing linen is all about making you more content with your surroundings.

► 4 5

tablecloth and napkins

♥

The textures and colors of the seaside were my inspiration for this unusual tablesetting, perfect for al fresco dining on hot summer days. The mood is restful, and redolent of lazy days spent barefoot, combing the beach for seashells. I chose a natural sand-colored linen to complement the shell motifs which are printed in a dark, maritime blue and white. Using a combination of stamping and stencilling techniques, as here, gives the design a characteristic fullness, and allows the details to be accentuated.

While closely woven fabric gives the clearest stencils, it is fun to experiment with the effects which can be achieved with different weaves and textures of fabric. In this instance, I was delighted with the way the fabric accepted the stamps and stencils: the slightly uneven effect adds yet another texture dimension.

Detail showing one shell stamp overlaid with a decorative stencil.

FABRIC

velvet stencilled
pillow

♥

Comfort and good looks are the two major factors to consider when planning the soft furnishings of a room. Unfortunately, even the most elegant sofa can be disappointingly stiff and unyielding. This is where the humble pillow comes in. A couple of plumped-up pillows can make all the difference on an uncomfortable couch, and can turn a cold armchair into a cosy nest you will be reluctant to leave.

In addition to their ability to bring comfort, pillows are also serve a decorative function: they can add a splash of color or bring together a daring mix of fabrics; they can blend in or make a strong statement. They can be firm or soft and squishy, large or small, and of course the variety of fabric and trimmings is endless: the decision is yours.

▶ 49

Choose any combination of stencils or one single motif to decorate the fabric surface.

I chose luxurious velvet in an antique gold as the fabric for this stencilling project. Velvet is always irresistible – warm and soft to the touch, it feels gloriously extravagant, yet it is not vastly expensive, especially when you buy it in small, remnant-sized quantities.

The strength of this design is in its subtlety. A scattering of small motifs stencilled on the velvet in clear fabric paint catch the light and create an interesting contrast in textures.

▶ 51

furniture

▶ 53

S tencilled painted furniture – along with stencilled wallpaper – reached a peak of popularity in the Europe of the 1800s. When the first settlers left for America, they took with them the technique of stencilling, and proceeded to decorate their rustic homes with remembered, much-loved designs.

Painted furniture is an ideal subject for stencilling and stamping, provided the surface is smooth and regular. Even the most tired piece of furniture can be improved with a coat of paint and the application of a stencil. Chairs, linen chests, tables and chests of drawers are most commonly favored with this kind of attention, but the list is almost inexhaustible: doors, kitchen cab-

inets, armoire doors, toyboxes, headboards, bathroom cabinets – even wooden panelling – are all suitable. Tape down the stencil to prevent it from shifting, keep the paint on the brush minimal, to prevent the paint from dripping, and even children can achieve satisfying results. Stamping requires a bit more skill, since the stamp needs to be placed accurately and cleanly for the best results. Stamping with potato, rubber or sponge on scrap paper and fabric can provide good practice.

The four projects selected for inclusion in this chapter satisfied the criteria of simple style, namely function, simplicity and style. A simple rectangular table is given a base coat in a neutral color, and is transformed into a faux mosaic tile table which would freshen up any bathroom or sun room. I chose blues, lilac and gray for my table, but fire or earth colors would

be exciting as well. An ordinary upright chair, the type that lurks in any large kitchen, is given a "brass stud" finish with the clever use of a dot stamp, and a fleur-de-lys stamp design brighten up a dull blanket chest. The stencilled chest of drawers – first whitewashed before a pretty laurel leaf motif is applied – makes a charming addition to a romantic bedroom.

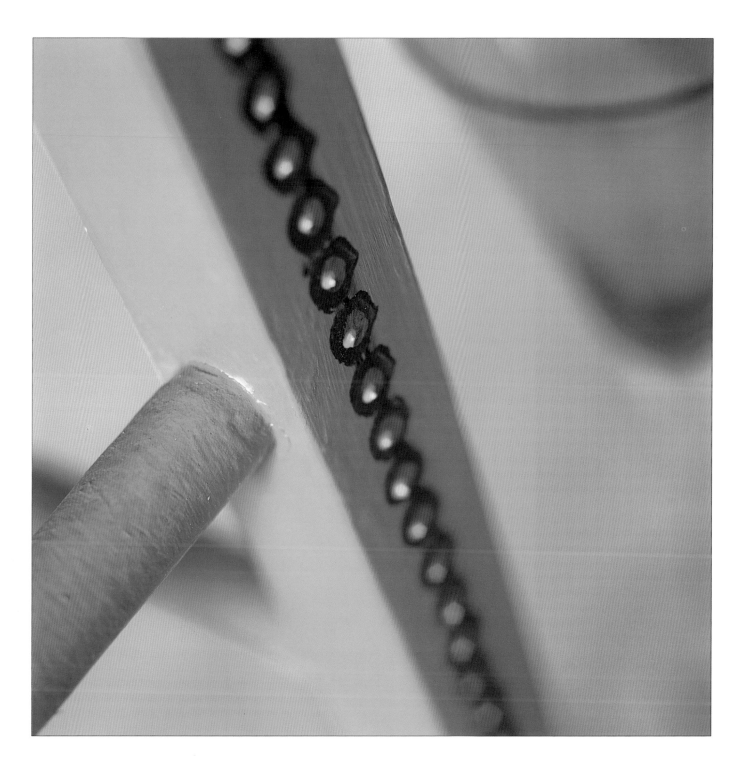

FURNITURE

stamped
blanket chest

♥

This blanket chest was a perfect subject for stencilling or stamping. The straightforward design, with its simple lines and smooth rectangular surfaces, would have worked well with any one of the stencil and stamp designs I considered. In the end, I used a traditional fleur-de-lys design, stamped in a formal pattern on each of the surfaces, with a contemporary, fresh color scheme of yellow and sage green. A navy blue tassel picks up the color of the fleur-de-lys and provides the finishing touch. The result has all the elements of simple style – simplicity, function and style – and I think you'll love it.

Classical motifs always work well. Keep the background color scheme minimal so the motif will stand out well.

laurel leaf
chest of drawers

♥

A chest of drawers is probably one item of furniture which is common to all our homes, and which will outlive our decorating fads and fancies. The chest of drawers purchased for the arrival of the new baby and carefully packed with tiny garments will, some years later, stand with drawers half open, stuffed with baggy sweat pants and tee-shirts. Gone will be the Peter Rabbit-type nursery curtains and lampshade, replaced by posters of current basketball stars and rock bands. But the chest of drawers need not be frozen in time. By stencilling on a design which reflects the age of the room's occupant, and which complements the decorative theme of the room, you can keep pace with evolving tastes without spending a fortune. This pretty chest of drawers, perfect for a feminine bedroom, was whitewashed before a laurel leaf design was stencilled on to it.

▶ 59

Clean simple lines complement the laurel leaf pattern on the corner of this chest of drawers.

mosaic
table top

♥

Magnificent mosaic: whether a classical piece gracing the floor of an ancient Venetian church, or a geometric design in the brightly-lit bathroom of a Las Vegas casino, mosaic is everywhere. It is an old and enduring art, loved as much for its vibrant colors as for its designs.

Here, I show you how you can create your own "mosaic" table top using the simple technique of stamping, without the bother of glass cutting, grouting or special tools; all you need is a mosaic tile-sized stamp, acrylic paint – and a steady hand. In fact, perhaps the most difficult part about making this table top is deciding on the colors for your "tiles." I chose a fresh blue/gray/lilac scheme, which is perfect for a bathroom setting. For a different room, say a sun room, I could have chosen a medley of greens, fire or earth colors.

FURNITURE

Once you have mastered the technique of applying the paint to the stamp to give an authentic mottled look – reminiscent of traditional Italian glass tiles – you might like to experiment with a black and white scheme, or even a pattern.

62 ◀

upholstery
tack chair

♥

A single straight-backed chair, the type you might pull up to the kitchen table when you stop for a coffee break, is often the orphan in home decorating. Now you can give that boring old chair a bit of attention with this clever idea. Using a dot stamp dipped in a rough blend of bronze and black paint to stamp rows of "metallic" dots, you can create a faux three-dimensional upholstery tack effect.

Once it has undergone its transformation, you won't want to put this chair behind the kitchen door out of sight; you'll want to find a place for it where it can be the focus of attention and admiration! In the hallway, perhaps, in the den, or maybe on the landing...?

▶ 65

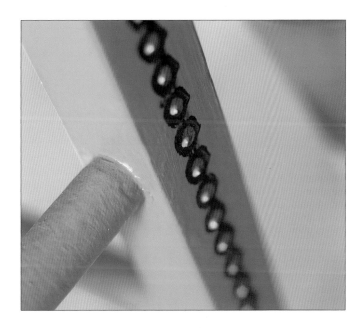

Close-up of the "metallic" dot pattern.

▶ 67

It is the small things, the little touches, which give any home its unique feel. The way we attend to the fine details around the home says more about us than weeks of painstaking wallpapering or a designer kitchen ever could. Perhaps this is because it is here where the decorating "buck" stops – these accessories, each carefully chosen from an often bewildering array of colors, styles and sizes, represent the very essence of our style. Simple style is all about getting rid of unnecessary clutter; paring back to simple, uncomplicated lines; using natural materials and the celebration of space. This does not exclude the use of accessories; on the contrary, when chosen and placed with care, accessories can enhance simple style through contrast, harmony and even humor. The technique of stencilling and stamping is an easy and effective way to personalize your purchased finds and, should you later wish to make an identical copy of an earlier creation, the technique, by its definition, allows you do just that. My choice of projects includes ideas for those hand-me-down items that we are all given when we set up home, but which need a personal stamp to make them our own.

The stencilling and stamping beginner will find that accessories are a good place to start, since most of the items are small and the financial outlay is modest. From a vast selection of possible projects, I have chosen four easy projects which are well within the reach of the novice: a glass bowl given star treatment; a pair of sophisticated "gilt" picture frames; a lampshade with an intriguing spiral design and a set of striped storage jars and labels for your kitchen. I hope success with these small projects will fire your creative spark and perhaps encourage you to develop your own ideas; any one of these stencilling ideas can be adapted to suit your own taste and needs.

ACCESSORIES

frosted glass
bowl

Glass is amazingly versatile. It can be cut, blown and molded into the most intricate shapes; it may be clear or opaque, colored or frosted; it can be functional or decorative, thick or thin. But, despite its potential, I suspect we all have some rather uninspiring glassware, possibly a vase or bowl, a pitcher, or even a set of glasses. In spite of its smooth surface, glass makes a very successful subject for stencils provided the stencil is taped down securely before you begin.

This bowl, stencilled with stars and filled with floating candles, makes a sparkling centerpiece for a special occasion, but it could just as well show off a delicious chocolate mousse or a festive selection of chocolates, nuts and dates. Deceptively simple to make, this bowl takes no more than an hour or two to complete.

▶ 71

Detail of a large frosted opaque star.

picture
frames

♥

A frame has the potential to "make or break" a picture. The picture which will stop you in mid-stride when mounted in an attractive frame may not get a second glance if mounted in a drab frame. Choosing a frame can be a frustrating exercise: you have in mind a style or finish which apparently has yet to be invented, let alone manufactured, and your aching feet will vouch for your lack of success. What are your options? Learning the skill of picture framing is certainly one alternative, but may be more of a commitment than you are ready to make. Another alternative is to buy a ready-made frame with a simple design, and decorate it to suit your needs.

72 ◄

Black and gold frames look elegant and stylish without detracting from the focus of the picture.

74

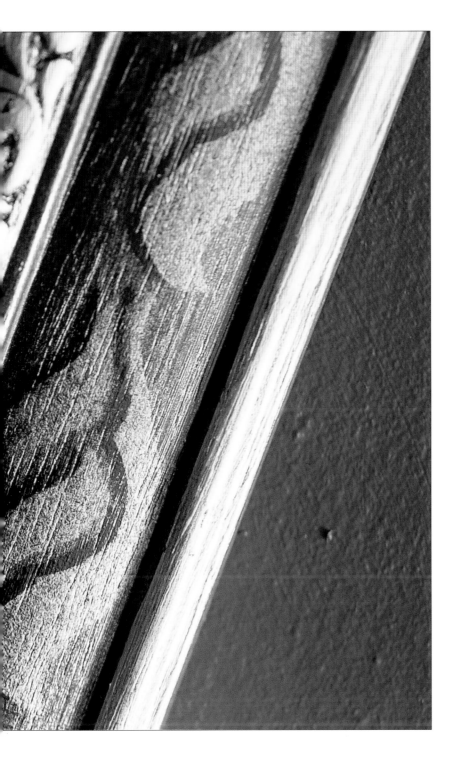

These elegant frames draw attention to the small pictures within, but, more than that, they are themselves works of art which will attract many admiring glances. Each was first painted with a base coat of black and then rubbed with a little gold metallic paste to enhance the pattern in relief. A border stencil was applied, first in black and then, moving the stencil slightly downwards, in gold paint, thus creating a drop shadow effect. This is an easy, but very rewarding, project.

▶ 7 5

string stamped
lampshade

♥

The ambiance of a room relies heavily on lighting. For mood lighting, it is often best to use individual lamps, or spot lights, and avoid the glare of general lighting. A lamp, placed nearby at the right height, can turn a comfortable chair into a favorite reading refuge, as well as a warm focus for the room.

When choosing a lampshade, make sure your shade width is in proportion to the height of the lamp-stand, to prevent a bottom-heavy or top-heavy look. Also, remember that the shape of the shade and its color will affect the amount and intensity of the light it will provide.

I have made more of this textured lampshade by simply stamping a repeating spiral design in a rich yellow ocher around the base. Try experimenting with color and texture, but bear in mind the silhouette effect on your design when the lamp is switched on.

storage jars
and labels

♥

A glance inside my kitchen cabinets reveals a motley collection of unsightly jars, cartons, tins and bags containing coffee, tea, rice, sugar and flour. My spice cabinet is worse – spice bottles of different sizes jostle for space, some knocked down in the crush – and finding the spice required for a recipe involves unpacking the cabinet and examining the bottles one by one. A storage nightmare, and the inspiration for this project.

With a bit of imagination, a pot of bright enamel paint, a stamp and some stencils, I have turned the kitchen storage problem into an asset. Blue-and-white striped storage jars announce their contents in clear black lettering, and spice bottles with attractive labels stand to attention in ordered rows. I think you will love these storage jars so much you'll want them on display, so bear that in mind when you choose your color scheme!

putting it together

The projects described in *Simple Stamps & Stencils Style* are all well within the reach of the average reader. The designs are simple and the materials required couldn't be more basic – principally paint, brushes, masking tape and a mixture of stencils or stamps. The templates for the stencils and stamps are printed on pages 104–111. Ready-made stencils and stamps are widely available from the larger home improvement stores and, increasingly, from special stencil/stamp stores, where the staff will be able to answer your questions and offer advice.

Making a stencil involves the transfer of a design onto the stencil material. For this, the easiest method is to use clear acetate, tracing paper or the photocopied design, a craft knife and a cutting mat, preferably of the self-healing variety. For a large design, simply tape pieces of clear plastic together to the required length. With clear plastic you can see exactly where you are placing your stencil and it is easy to transfer your designs onto it.

Trace the outline of your chosen design, or alternately photocopy your own choice of motif. Tape the image to the cutting mat so that it does not shift. Now secure the plastic on top. Holding the blade away from you, carefully cut out the stencil using a craft knife. It is important that you cut cleanly without going over the design lines, as any irregularities will affect the clarity of your stencil. Don't forget to include strengthening "bridges" if you are designing your own stencil.

Stamps are cut from foam or rubber which can then be glued to a block of wood for easy handling. Wood allows an even pressure to be applied when stamping. High density (condensed) foam rubber is good for detailed designs, while low density, synthetic foam, such as a bath sponge, gives a rougher result. When using foam rubber, trace designs off the source using tracing paper and then use spray adhesive

to attach the tracing to the foam. Cut out using a craft knife. Low density foam is too soft for tracing purposes. Instead, draw freehand designs onto the foam using a water-based marker, then cut out the shape using sharp scissors. Rinse out all traces of the marker pen.

The secret of stencilling and stamping is in the controlled use of paint. Always begin by pouring a little paint onto a plate. For stamping, use a small roller or a brush to apply paint to the stamp, then press the stamp firmly onto the required surface. For stencilling, dip the tip of the brush into the paint and blot off the excess on a cloth or paper towel. You should aim to have a brush which is almost dry. Hold the brush perpendicular to

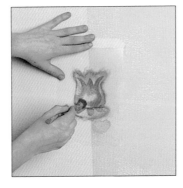

the surface and, working away from the edges towards the center of the stencil, apply the paint, building up the color gradually. Stippling or dabbing, flicking and rotating the brush all give different results. If paint bleeds under the edge of the stencil, you have used too much. Some people prefer to use oil-based paint sticks, which are "drier" than paint, and some use sponges to apply the paint. Try out different methods on scrap paper first until you are comfortable with a technique that suits your needs. In general solvent-based paints are not recommended since they distort or melt stencil materials.

You will want to re-use a favorite stencil, and often stencils need to be reversed to achieve the inverse of the design, so it is vital to clean your stencils well after use. If you are covering large wall or floor surfaces, cut extra stencils before you begin, so that damaged or scratched stencils can be dis-

carded and replaced quickly without hindering the work in progress. Adequate preparation will always ensure better results and less wasted time. Wipe off water-based paint by soaking the plastic in warm soapy water. Clean your brushes after stencilling, either in warm, soapy water or solvent, then rinse and leave to dry. Once dry, use a loosely-tied elastic band to keep the bristles in shape.

checked stamped floor

♥

Give your room a new look with this fresh floor design in the crisp colors of early spring.

84 ◀

MATERIALS

Quantities given are for an average-sized room.

◆ *3/4 gallon/2.5 liters pale gray/mauve paint in eggshell finish for base coat*
◆ *1/4 gallon/1 liter pale yellow paint in eggshell finish*
◆ *1/4 gallon/1 liter cream paint in eggshell finish*
◆ *1/4 gallon/1 liter lilac paint in eggshell finish*
◆ *1/4 gallon/1 liter mauve paint in eggshell finish*
◆ *Four 1in/2.5cm brushes*
◆ *Two square stamps: one 4in/10cm, one 8in/20cm*

1 Remove flaking paint and old varnish from the wooden floorboard surface. Then sand, prime and give the floor an undercoat. Oil-based paints are best for floors as they are durable and therefore withstand heavy traffic.

2 For this floor, apply a liberal base coat of pale gray/mauve to the prepared floorboards.

3 Dab cream and pale yellow onto a large, square stamp without blending them too much.

4 Begin stamping the floor along the edge and, once you have completed one row, use the last stamp as a positioning guide.

5 Dab two colors (lilac and mauve) onto the smaller square stamp, being careful not to blend them too much.

6 Position over the intersection of the larger squares and stamp.

leaf stamped whitewashed floor

♥

Create a truly contemporary appearance with whitewashed floorboards stamped with a leaf design.

MATERIALS
Quantities given are suitable for an average-sized room.
- ¼ gallon/1 liter blue/gray paint with eggshell/satin finish for "ageing" base coat
- ¼ gallon/1 liter lime white paint with eggshell/satin finish
- Leaf-shaped stamps cut from foam rubber (see page 107)
- 27fl.oz/750ml gloss varnish
- 2in/5cm paint brush
- Paint bucket
- Cloth
- Mineral spirits
- Container
- Small roller

1 Prepare the floor as described on page 84, step 1. Age new floorboards like these with a base coat wash made from one part blue/gray paint mixed with three parts mineral spirits. Leave to dry thoroughly.

2 Pour a small amount of gloss varnish into a container. Pick up a small amount on the roller and apply an even coat to a leaf stamp.

3 To make a border around the room, apply different leaf stamps 6in/15cm away from the skirting board, changing the angle of each print as desired. Allow to dry thoroughly before proceeding to the next step.

4 Apply a whitewash made of one part whitewash paint and four parts mineral spirits. Brush on evenly in the direction of the grain.

5 Once the wash has begun to soak into the wood, wipe over the stamps with a clean cloth. The leaf shapes will become visible as the paint dries.

green gingham floor

♥

This cool green gingham floor is perfect for a sun room or kitchen – and it is surprisingly simple to do.

MATERIALS

Quantities given are for an average-sized room.

◆ *¾ gallon/2.5 liters lime white paint in eggshell finish for base coat*

◆ *¼ gallon/1 liter mid-green paint in eggshell finish*

◆ *¼ gallon/1 liter darker green paint in eggshell finish*

◆ *Pencil and large ruler*

◆ *Stencil 12in/30cm square*

◆ *1in/2.5cm brush*

1 Prepare the floor as described on page 84 (checked stamped floor), step 1.

2 Apply a base coat in lime white eggshell paint.

3 The width of each plank will determine the size of the squares. Using a large ruler placed against the edge of each plank to achieve a sharp edge, stipple mid-green paint down the length of every other plank. Repeat until all the stripes in one direction are complete.

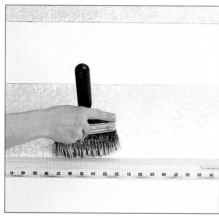

4 Measure the width of the planks and, using these measurements, stipple mid-green paint across in the opposite direction to form a grid pattern.

5 Using a stencil cut to the size of the square at the intersections, stipple a square of darker green.

nautical rope twist floor

♥

Bring the feel of the sea and the creak of the wooden deck to your bathroom with this nautical floor decoration

MATERIALS
Quantities given are suitable for an average-sized room.
◆ *¾ gallon/2.5 liters white paint in eggshell finish for base coat*
◆ *9fl.oz/250ml dark blue paint in eggshell finish*
◆ *Pencil and ruler*
◆ *Masking tape*
◆ *Stencil brush*
◆ *Two rope twist stencils (see page 105)*
◆ *Paint brush*

1 Prepare the floor as described on page 84 (checked stamped floor), step 1.

2 Apply a base coat using white eggshell paint.

3 Using a pencil and ruler, measure and draw a guideline around the edge of the floor.

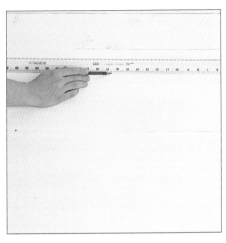

4 Begin at a corner with the narrow rope twist stencil and stipple a little dark blue paint along the edge of the stencil to create a shade effect. Continue until the border is complete, except for the corner gaps.

5 Now, working with the wider stencil and using the same technique, position and stencil a second border within the first and a small distance from it. Continue until the second border is complete, except for the corner gaps.

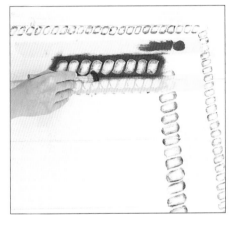

6 Mark off the gaps in the corners with masking tape. Lightly stipple using the same blue paint.

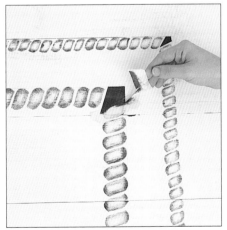

spiral wall finish

♥

Scrolls and rosettes offer a classical appearance which is enhanced by the cool blue and white color scheme.

MATERIALS

Quantities given are suitable for an average-sized room.
- *¾ gallon/2.5 liters powder blue flat latex paint for base coat*
- *¼ gallon/1 liter white flat latex paint*
- *Household sponge*
- *Stencil brush*
- *Stencil (see page 105)*
- *Masking tape and tape measure*
- *Pencil and level*
- *Cloth*
- *Length of wood the height of the wall between the baseboard and cornice*

1 Remove any dirt, dust and flaking paint from the wall.

2 Dip one side of the household sponge into the powder blue latex paint. Wipe off the excess on the side of the can. To cre-ate a soft mottled paint effect, using the sponge, apply the paint onto the wall using a circular motion. Once dry, any uneven areas can be buffed over with a small amount of paint.

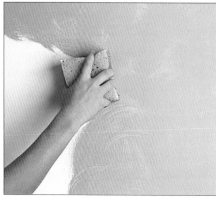

3 Working across the wall from left ot right, mark points 12in/30cm apart.

4 Tape a level to the wood and draw a vertical line through every marked point as a guide for the stencil.

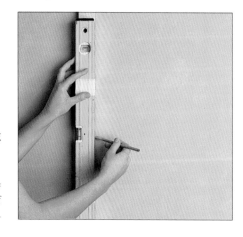

5 Apply masking tape to each end of the stencil. Place the stencil at the top of the wall, aligning the top edge with the pencil line.

6 Dip the stencil brush into white paint and wipe off any excess onto a cloth or paper towel to prevent any paint from creeping under the stencil. Apply the paint by stippling.

7 Peel the stencil away from the wall from the bottom upwards, to prevent any smearing. Alternate the design by turning the cleaned stencil upside down.

plaster spot wall finish

♥

This unusual paint and plaster application is quick to apply, fast-drying and creates a very attractive finish for a plastered wall.

MATERIALS
Quantities given are suitable for an average-sized room.
- ¾ gallon/2.5 liters stone green flat latex paint
- ¾ gallon/2.5 liters plaster white flat latex paint
- Powder spackle
- Paintbrushes
- Small sponge roller
- Medium artist's brush

1 Remove any dirt, dust and flaking paint from the wall.

2 Brush the wall with a base coat of green and allow to dry.

3 Apply a generous coat of plaster white latex paint over the green base coat in random, sweeping strokes. Do not cover the green entirely – the random appearance will create a rough plaster look.

4 Mix the plaster white latex paint with spackle – one part paint to one part filler. Dab a small amount onto one end of the roller. Firmly press the roller onto the wall in the required position until the mixture is pushed out to the edges of the roller. Space plaster circles over the wall.

5 Rotate the tip of an artist's brush in a circular motion in the middle of the stamp to flatten any bumps in the mixture where the roller was pulled away from the wall. Allow to dry thoroughly.

initial letter monogram

♥

This sophisticated design is a remarkably simple, yet striking, example of the versatile art of stencilling. Applied in two stages, to build up the shadow effect, this stencil idea will give a wall a truly personal touch.

MATERIALS

Quantities given are suitable for an average-sized room.
- *¾ gallon/2.5 liters burgundy red latex paint*
- *Small can ultramarine blue acrylic paint*
- *Small can gold acrylic paint*
- *Small can silver acrylic paint*
- *Masking tape*
- *Three stencil brushes*
- *Two-layer monogram stencil (see page 109–111)*

1 Remove any dirt, dust and flaking paint from the wall.

2 Apply a base coat of burgundy red latex paint to the wall surface.

3 Place the first layer of the stencil in position on the wall. Using a stencil brush, stipple in ultramarine blue paint.

4 Using a second brush, paint the decorative leaves in gold. Allow to dry.

5 Carefully position the second layer of the stencil to fit over the first. Using silver paint, stencil the letter, then flick paint inwards from the end of each border line.

6 Stipple the decorative leaves in gold as before.

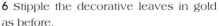

tulip wall panel
♥

Make much more of a special antique shop find, or give a dull alcove a treat with this unusual wall treatment.

MATERIALS
Quantities given are suitable for an average-sized room.
- ¾ gallon/2.5 liters ice blue latex paint for the base coat
- ¼ gallon/1 liter cream latex paint
- Small can sage green acrylic paint
- Small can pale green acrylic paint
- Small can dark red acrylic paint
- Tulip stencil and border (see page 108)
- Wallpaper paste
- Masking tape
- Three stencil brushes
- Level
- Ruler

1 Ensure that the surface is free of dirt and dust, and that any flaking paint has been removed. Latex, acrylic and stencil paints are all suitable for use on plaster walls.

2 Using a sponge, apply a base coat of ice blue latex paint to create a soft, mottled effect.

3 Using the level and ruler, mark out the panel, making sure that its proportions balance with the room. Mask off the panel with masking tape.

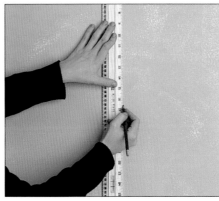

4 Mix cream latex paint with wallpaper paste in a ratio of 1:1, and apply to the panel with a large brush in a vertical dragging motion.

5 Find the center point of each side of the panel and stencil a tulip head over each mark. Make sure the tulip head remains upright on all four sides.

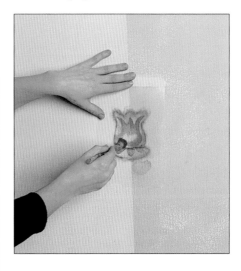

6 Working away from the tulip head, stencil the border first in one direction. Clean the stencil thoroughly, then flip it over in the other direction to produce the mirror image.

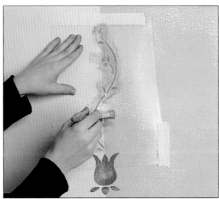

feather stencilled curtain

♥

Transform your plain curtains with this delicate feather motif – all you need is fabric paint, brushes and a stencil.

MATERIALS

Quantities given are suitable for one pair of curtains.

◆ *One pair of navy blue ready-made curtains*

◆ *Two small cans white fabric paint*

◆ *Small can pale blue fabric paint*

◆ *Masking tape*

◆ *Cardboard*

◆ *Feather stencil (see page 108)*

◆ *Two stencil brushes*

1 Wash and iron the curtains to remove any starch and to allow for shrinkage.

2 Protect your working surface. Smooth out the fabric onto a table top and place a piece of cardboard under the area to be stencilled. Hold the fabric in place using strips of masking tape.

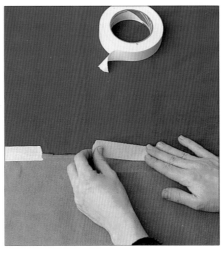

3 Hold the stencil in position and stipple with white fabric paint.

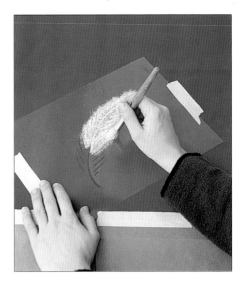

4 Using a second brush and pale blue paint, apply paint to the feather tips.

ice poppies bed linen

♥

Cut your own floral pattern from a piece of foam rubber to make an original stencil design, or choose a motif that will coordinate with wall coverings and window treatments.

MATERIALS

Quantities given are suitable for a single duvet cover and one pillowcase.

◆ *Single duvet cover and one pillow-case in white Egyptian cotton*
◆ *Two small cans pale blue fabric paint*
◆ *Small can white fabric paint*
◆ *Small can green fabric paint*
◆ *Flower-shaped stamp cut from foam rubber (see page 107)*
◆ *Small roller*
◆ *Cardboard*
◆ *Container*
◆ *Selection of artist's and stencil brushes*
◆ *Masking tape*

1 Iron the duvet cover and pillowcase. Place a piece of cardboard under the top layer of fabric to prevent the paint from printing onto the layer below.

2 Tape the edges of the pillowcase to the work surface to create a frame within which to print the stamps.

3 Pour a small quantity of light blue fabric paint into a container and, using a roller, apply a thin layer to the surface of the stamp.

4 Apply white paint to the flower center using an artist's brush or stencil brush. Press the stamp firmly onto the fabric in the required position.

5 Repeating steps 3 and 4, randomly cover the surface of the pillowcase, allowing sufficient space between each flower for the stems.

► 93

6 With a fine artist's brush and green paint, paint the stem for each flower.

7 Complete the top surface of the duvet cover in the same way, but, for the underside, apply closely-spaced flower heads without stems.

tablecloth and napkins

♥

The colors, textures and images of the seaside were the inspiration for this table linen which combines the techniques of stamping and stencilling.

MATERIALS
Quantities given are approximate and depend on the size of the tablecloth and napkins.
◆ *Tablecloth and napkins in natural linen*
◆ *Small can white fabric paint*
◆ *Small can dark blue fabric paint*
◆ *Shell stamps and stencils (see page 109)*
◆ *Masking tape*
◆ *Cardboard*
◆ *Fine artist's brush and stencil brush*
◆ *Small roller*
◆ *Palette*

1 Wash and iron the fabric to remove any starch and to allow for shrinkage.

2 Smooth the fabric onto a flat surface and place a piece of cardboard under the area to be stamped.

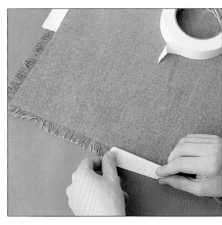

3 Pour a little white fabric paint onto a palette and, using the roller, apply a good amount onto the shell stamp. Place the stamp in position at the corner of the fabric and stamp firmly. Stamp all four corners then position and stamp the border. Allow to dry.

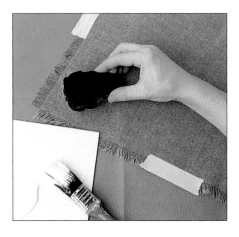

4 Carefully place the shell stencil over the stamp. Dip the tip of the stencil brush in dark blue paint and flick inwards from the edge of the stencil. Do not cover the white completely.

5 Using a fine artist's brush and dark blue paint, add a line of definition around each shell.

velvet stencilled pillow

A scattering of small stencils in clear fabric paint emphasizes the sumptuous textures of these velvet pillows. Choose a stencil design to complement your existing theme.

▶ 95

1 Make your template from the pattern provided on page 107.

2 Place a piece of cardboard inside the pillow cover to avoid printing through both layers of the fabric.

3 Secure the pillow cover by taping it to the work surface.

4 Position the stencil and stipple with clear fabric paint.

5 When stencilling at the edge, position the stencil so that it overlaps the side and then stipple as before.

6 Once the stencilling is complete and the paint is dry, sew on the braid.

MATERIALS

Quantities given are suitable for at least two medium-sized pillows.

- ◆ *Pair of antique gold velvet pillows*
- ◆ *Medium can clear fabric paint*
- ◆ *Stencil brush*
- ◆ *Stencil (see page 107)*
- ◆ *Masking tape*
- ◆ *Cardboard*
- ◆ *Selection of braids*
- ◆ *Template*

stamped blanket chest

♥

Choose a stencil motif and color scheme to complement your room and turn a functional piece of furniture like this blanket chest into a showpiece.

MATERIALS

Quantities given are approximate and depend on the size of the piece of furniture.

◆ *Blanket chest or other suitable wooden box*
◆ *¼ gallon/1 liter sage green oil-based paint for the base coat*
◆ *9fl.oz/250ml dark yellow paint with eggshell finish*
◆ *Small can navy blue acrylic paint*
◆ *Fleur-de-lys stamp (see page 107)*
◆ *Small roller*
◆ *Artist's brush*
◆ *1in/2.5cm brush*
◆ *Pencil and ruler*
◆ *Masking tape*

1 Sand off any flaking paint and old varnish from the surface. Apply a base coat of sage green paint.

2 Using a pencil and ruler, measure and draw a border with indented corners.

3 Mask off the area and dry brush dark yellow eggshell paint across the panel. Remove the masking tape carefully as soon as you finish.

4 Lightly brush over the surface of the box with sage green, so that the yellow shows through.

5 Using the roller, apply navy blue paint to the stamp. Place the stamp in position at the corner and stamp firmly. Repeat at each corner.

6 Using an artist's brush and blue paint, carefully add a blue line around the edge of each panel.

laurel leaf chest of drawers

This fresh and feminine chest of drawers is no more than a weekend's work. Choose a simple motif like this laurel leaf and keep to one or two tones of the same color for fuss-free results.

MATERIALS

Quantities given are approximate and depend on the size of the piece of furniture.

◆ *Wooden chest of drawers*
◆ *¼ gallon/1 liter whitewash paint in eggshell finish for base coat*
◆ *Small can light green acrylic paint*
◆ *Small can mid-green acrylic paint*
◆ *Laurel leaf stencil (see page 106)*
◆ *2in/5cm brush*
◆ *Pencil and ruler*
◆ *Masking tape*

1 Sand off any flaking paint and old varnish from the surface. Using whitewash paint as a base coat, dry brush each side of the chest of drawers in the direction of the grain.

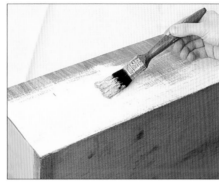

2 Using a pencil and ruler, measure and draw a center line across the depth and width of each drawer as a guide for stencilling. Position the leaf stencil. Using mid-green acrylic paint, stencil the leaf stalk and flick the brush from the base of each leaf upwards.

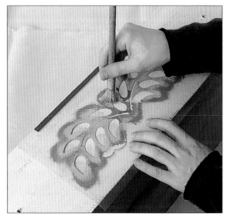

3 Then, using light green paint, flick from the top of each leaf downwards.

4 Paint a border line in light green around the drawer front. Mask off the central leaf, position on each corner and stencil as before.

mosaic table top

♥

Give a table a faux mosaic tile finish that is fresh, stylish and practical. This one looks stunning in the bathroom, but it would look just as good in the sun room or kitchen. Experiment with color and enjoy yourself!

MATERIALS

Quantities given are approximate and depend on the size of the furniture.

◆ *Small wooden table*
◆ *¼ gallon/1 liter pale beige oil-based paint for under coat*
◆ *Small can lilac acrylic paint*
◆ *Small can pale gray acrylic paint*
◆ *Small can pale blue acrylic paint*
◆ *Small can mid-blue acrylic paint*
◆ *Mosaic stamp (see page 106)*
◆ *Small brushes*
◆ *Varnish*
◆ *Cardboard*

1 Prepare the wood before you begin. Sand off any flaking paint and old varnish and apply an undercoat.

2 Apply a base coat of pale beige to the table top.

3 Dab several colors of acrylic paint onto a piece of cardboard, taking care not to blend them together too much.

4 Dip the stamp in the paint. Starting in one corner of the table top, press the stamp down firmly.

5 Using the previous stamp as a guide, continue across the table top, leaving a "grout" line between each stamp.

6 For the edge, hold the top of the stamp at each end and print a line of "tiles" along the side.

7 Apply a final protective coat of varnish if the area you are working on is to be used on a daily basis.

upholstery tack chair

♥

This simple straight-backed chair has been given a smart new look with this deceptively easy "upholstery tack" stamp finish.

MATERIALS

Quantities given are approximate and depend on the size of the furniture.

◆ *Straight-backed wooden chair*
◆ *¼ gallon/1 liter dark turquoise oil-based paint for base coat*
◆ *Small can black acrylic paint*
◆ *Small can bronze acrylic paint*
◆ *Small can light bronze acrylic paint*
◆ *Small can gold relief paint*
◆ *Small brush*
◆ *Pencil and ruler*
◆ *⅓ in/1cm diameter circle stamp*
◆ *Palette*

1 Prepare the wood as described on page 98, step 1. Apply a base coat of dark turquoise paint.

2 Draw a pencil guide line along the center of each strut.

3 Pour black and bronze paint onto a palette, without blending the colors too much. Dab the stamp into the paint and begin stamping over the line. Proceed along the line, placing each stamp up against the previous one, keeping the spacing tight.

4 Using a small brush and light bronze paint, add a dot to each stamp.

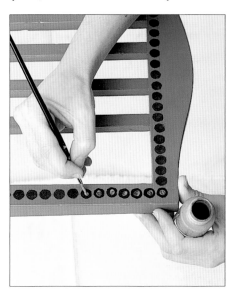

5 To add highlights, add a dot of gold relief paint straight from the tube, just off-center over each stamp.

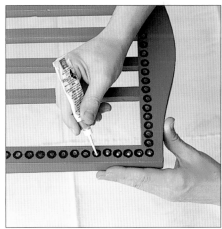

frosted glass bowl

♥

Floating candles illuminate this star-spangled bowl, making it a festive centerpiece for a celebration meal. When stencilling onto glassware, it is important to use glass paints, since normal latex paints and acrylics will not adhere and are therefore not suitable.

MATERIALS
- ◆ *Glass bowl of suitable design*
- ◆ *Small can of glass frosting paint*
- ◆ *Stencil brush*
- ◆ *Two star stencils: one large, one smaller (see page 107)*
- ◆ *Masking tape*
- ◆ *Soapy water*
- ◆ *Lint-free cloth*

1 Clean the glass thoroughly in warm soapy water and dry with a lint-free cloth.

2 Make sure the glass is completely dry and free from dust before you begin stencilling.

3 Tape the larger star stencil into position using masking tape. Stipple with frosting paint. Repeat, spacing the large star at random around the bowl. Allow to dry.

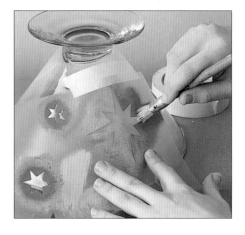

4 Fill in any gaps as desired using the smaller star stencil.

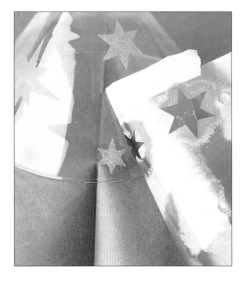

picture frames

♥

These simple frames have been given a metallic sheen and an interesting drop shadow border.

1 Paint the frame with black satin paint as a base coat. Allow to dry.

2 Rub a little gold metallic paste over the surface to leave a metallic sheen.

3 Tape the border stencil in position along the outer edge of the frame and stipple using black satin finish. Allow to dry.

4 Move the stencil slightly upwards. Stipple using gold acrylic paint. This will create a drop shadow effect.

MATERIALS

Quantities given are approximate and depend on the size of the frames.

◆ *Wooden picture frames*
◆ *9fl.oz/250ml black paint with satin finish for base coat*
◆ *Small can gold metallic paste*
◆ *Small can gold acrylic paint*
◆ *Masking tape*
◆ *Border stencil (see page 106)*
◆ *Two stencil brushes*
◆ *1in/2.5cm brush*

string stamped lampshade

♥

Design and make your own unique stamp for this lampshade project. Here, the string stamp complements the texture of the lampshade fabric, but you can adapt the design to suit your own requirements.

MATERIALS
Quantities given are suitable for a medium-sized lampshade.
- ◆ *Burgundy self-colored lampshade*
- ◆ *Small can yellow ocher acrylic paint*
- ◆ *Cardstock*
- ◆ *Glue*
- ◆ *Pencil*
- ◆ *String*
- ◆ *Small roller*

1 Draw a scroll shape onto a small square of cardstock (see page 107).

2 Pipe glue over the pencil guideline.

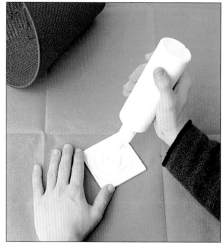

3 Starting in the center, curl a length of string around the glue scroll, pressing

the string into the glue as you work. Cut off the excess. Allow the stamp to dry.

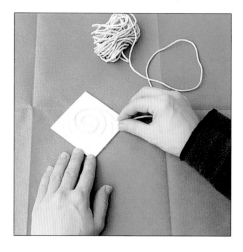

4 Using a small roller, apply yellow ocher paint to the stamp.

5 Carefully stamp onto the lower edge of the lampshade. Repeat until the border detail is complete.

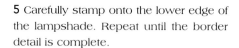

storage jars and labels

♥

Adapt this attractive storage solution to suit the color scheme of your kitchen. When stencilling onto ceramicware, it is important to use enamel paints, since normal latex paints and acrylics will not adhere and are therefore not suitable.

MATERIALS

Quantities given are approximate and depend on the size and number of jars and labels.

◆ *Selection of storage jars and spice bottles*
◆ *Small can navy blue enamel paint*
◆ *9fl.oz/250ml mid-blue enamel paint*
◆ *Small can black enamel paint*
◆ *Label stamp (see page 104)*
◆ *1in/2.5cm wide masking tape*
◆ *Lettering stencil (see page 104)*
◆ *Stencil brush and small roller*
◆ *White self-adhesive labels to fit spice bottles*

1 For the labels, using the roller, apply navy blue paint to the label stamp. Print onto the self-adhesive labels

2 Cut out along the outside edge of the blue border.

3 For the storage jars, fix masking tape in horizontal bands around each jar, allowing a 1in/2.5cm gap of white between the bands of tape.

4 Paint the gaps between masking tape bands in mid-blue enamel paint. Paint in the direction of the tape – using horizontal brush strokes. Completely cover any white areas. Allow to dry

5 Place the lettering stencil in position and stipple in black enamel paint.

templates

stencil

storage jars and labels
Actual size

stamp

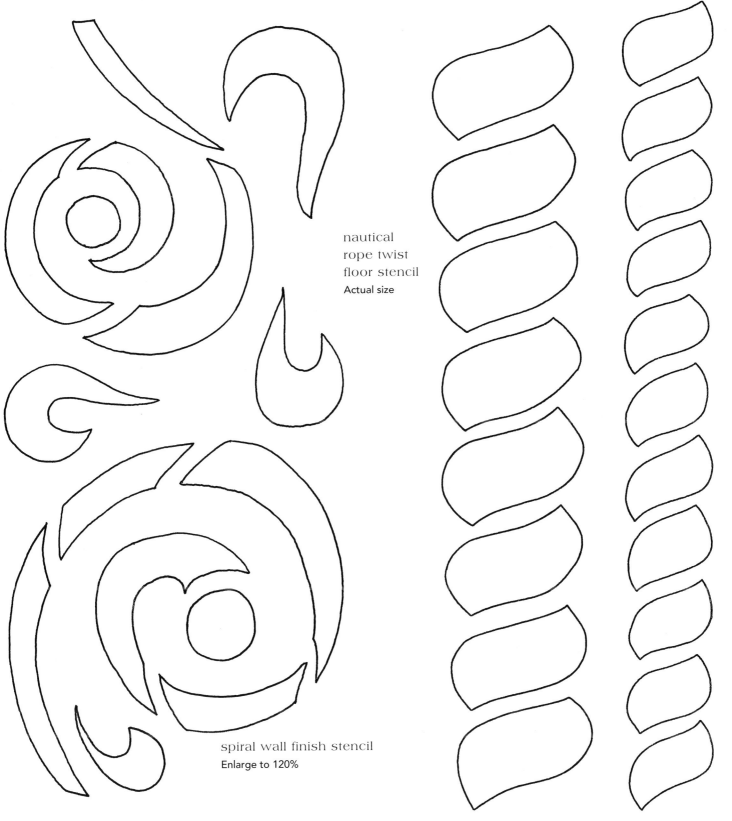

nautical
rope twist
floor stencil
Actual size

spiral wall finish stencil
Enlarge to 120%

TEMPLATES

laurel leaf chest of
drawers stencil
Actual size
**Reverse the image at the
broken line**

mosaic
table top
stamp
Actual size

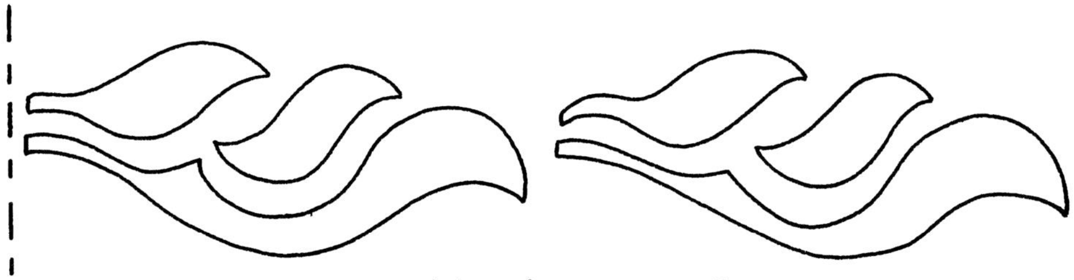

picture frames stencil
Actual size
Reverse the image at the broken line

leaf stamped floor
Actual size

ice poppies bed linen stamp
Actual size

frosted glass bowl stencil
Actual size

velvet
stencilled
pillow
Actual size

stamped blanket chest
Actual size

string stamped lampshade
Actual size

tulip wall panel
stencils
Actual size

feather
stencilled curtain
Actual size

tablecloth and napkins

Actual size. The stamp is defined by the blue line.
The stencil is defined by the black lines

First layer

initial letter monogram stencil

Actual size

Second layer

For the remaining initials see pages 110–111 and
enlarge them on a photocopier to 250%

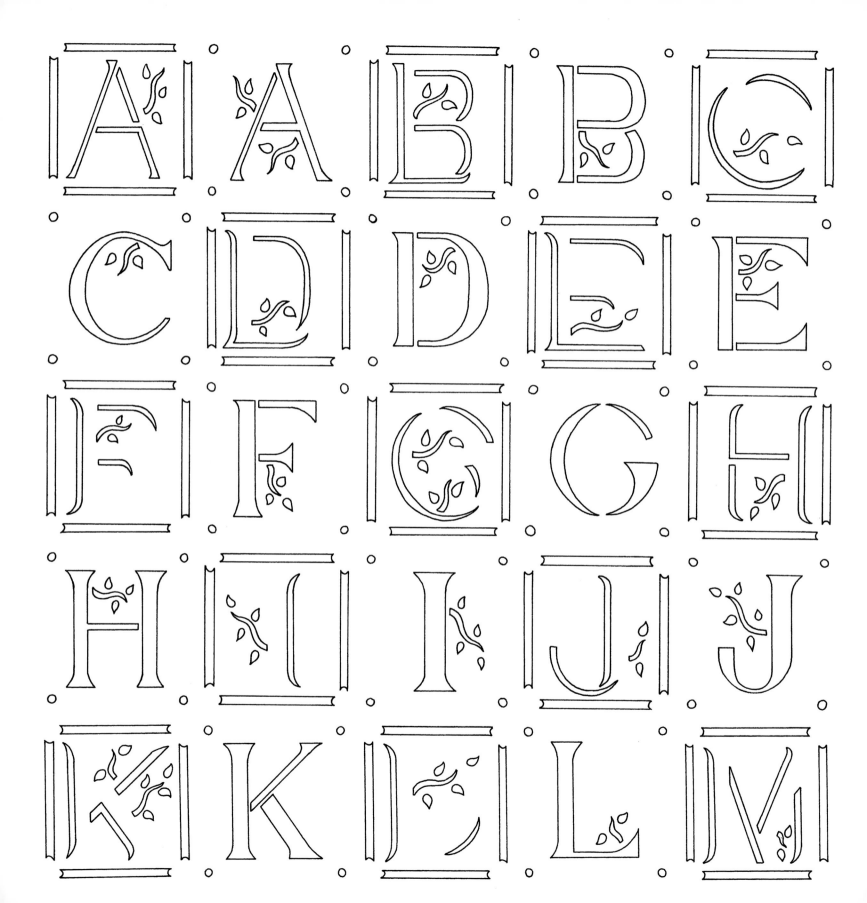

index